WHAT DOES IT MEAN TO BE A CHRISTIAN

WRITTEN BY ~ STEVEN LAKE

SPECIAL THANKS TO

I would like to thank Pastor Richard Wilson, as well as Sam and Savannah Jezowski, for their help in proofreading and editing the manuscript for this booklet. Their help, along with God's leading, has made this booklet possible

WHAT DOES IT MEAN TO BE A CHRISTIAN?

What does it mean to be a Christian? Is it being part of the largest social club on Earth, or part of a congregation or even attending church regularly? Is it someone who is narrow minded and bigoted, lost in their own world of wistful fantasy and Gaelic revelry? Or perhaps someone who lives in gilded castles and dreams of one day walking on white puffy clouds lined with glistening silver while floating on angel's wings as they strum their harps of gold?

Depending on who you ask, the answers can vary. Some see Christians as idealists while others view them as the most hateful people on the planet, or even the most foolish and misguided. i.e. the religion of the dumb. But is it? What is Christianity really? Well, first we have to understand what the name implies. First off, the name "Christian" is an adjective which identifies the individual with Jesus Christ, the object, focus and center of Christianity. Therefore to be a Christian is to be a follower of Christ Himself. Our Sin

To understand what makes a person a Christian, we first have to go back to the source of our problem. Namely, our sin. We, as human beings, are depraved, sinful creatures. To understand the depth of one's sin is to understand the sheer, unfathomable depravity of even the best we have to offer before God. Yes, to God, even our best, most righteous, most exceptional of all good deeds are evil, vile, disgusting and depraved.

But that still doesn't answer the question of what it truly means to be a Christian. Being named such is so much more than simply identifying with Jesus Christ, the Son of God. Because it's not WHO someone is that makes them a Christian, but WHAT they are. Allow me to explain.

OUR SIN

To understand what makes a person a Christian, we first have to go back to the source of our problem. Namely, our sin. We, as human beings, are depraved, sinful creatures. To understand the depth of one's sin is to understand the sheer, unfathomable depravity of even the best we have to offer before God. Yes, to God, even our best, most righteous, most exceptional of all good deeds are evil, vile, disgusting and depraved.

Isaiah 64:6 (KJV) - "*But we are all as an unclean thing, and all our righteousnesses are as filthy rags; and we all do fade as a leaf; and our iniquities, like the wind, have taken us away.*"

To understand this verse properly we must first go much, much deeper than simply the words given above. The reason why is because, to the modern person, the term "filthy rags" doesn't elicit the same reaction of utter and total revulsion the original author intended to convey. In the original Greek, the word for "filthy rags" is "ayd" which refers to a woman's "period" or menstrual flux, and was the most vile, disgusting, horrific, gut wrenching thing the Jewish people of the time knew. Especially those with extensive knowledge of the Levitical code. To others however, different imagery was used. For example, when addressing the church at Philippi, Paul chose to use the word "skubalon", which is Greek for dung or excrement. This is seen in Philippians 3:5-8.

Philippians 3:5-8 (KJV) - *"Circumcised the eighth day, of the stock of Israel, of the tribe of Benjamin, an Hebrew of the Hebrews; as touching the law, a Pharisee; Concerning zeal, persecuting the church; touching the righteousness which is in the law, blameless. But what things were gain to me, those I counted loss for Christ. Yea doubtless, and I count all things but loss for the excellency of the knowledge of Christ Jesus my Lord: for whom I have suffered the loss of all things, and do count them but **dung**, that I may win Christ,"*

So if you picture for yourself the most vile, wretched, disgusting, horrid, putrid thing you can imagine, you're only just beginning to understand the full measure of how utterly evil and depraved our good deeds are before God. Now, if our "good" deeds are that horrible, imagine just how utterly vile and repulsive our sins and rebellion are in God's eyes. Suddenly even our best deeds no longer look so good, do they? This in turn proves the simple fact that we, in and of ourselves, can't ever hope to come close to matching up to God's holiness. But this now begs another question. Is sin inherent,

or is it a choice? I believe it's both. Allow me to explain.
Psalm 51:5 (NIV) - *"Surely I was sinful at birth, sinful from the time my mother conceived me."*

When we are born, we come into this world with an inherited sin nature. We don't ask for it. It's just a part of who we are. But like our hair, our eyes and our entire body, we inherit our parents traits, as well as all of those from everyone before them leading all the way back to Adam, the first man in all of history. Therefore all are sinful at birth. Every single person. Thus no single human being, no matter how great or small they may be, is sinless.

Hebrews 10:26 (KJV) - *"For if we sin willfully after that we have received the knowledge of the truth, there remaineth no more sacrifice for sins."*

If we sin willfully? If? That certainly sounds like it's saying that it will happen, should we choose to do so. And there are plenty of examples in the Bible and real life of men and women who had the choice to do good or evil, and instinctively chose evil. But since it's a choice and we can do either good or evil, the decision to sin is thus also a willful choice. As such sin is both inherited (i.e. we're born with the nature that instinctively leans towards evil) and intentional. It'd be one thing if you had no control over whether you sinned or not. If it was not your choice, then it is unlikely that God would hold it against you as you would not be responsible for your actions. However, since it *is* willful, we are held fully accountable for every sin we commit. So it is both our sin nature and our willful desire to sin that has made us who we are.

Romans 3:10 (KJV) - *"As it is written, There is none righteous, no, not one:"*

Because of these two states, both inherited and willful sin, everyone on this planet, from Adam to present, is guilty of sin. But wait a second, doesn't that mean that the very man we follow, Jesus Christ, is also guilty of sin? No, because Jesus was not born of man, but of woman. Now you're probably sitting there completely confused saying, "Aren't we all born from women?" Yes, our mothers give birth to us. However, this is speaking of the source of our identity and of who we are. In biblical terms the man was the source of life, because without his sperm (aka, "seed" in the Bible), a child was not possible. And it is through Adam that all sin has come and been passed down.

Romans 5:15 (ESV) - *"But the free gift is not like the trespass. For if many died through one man's trespass, much more have the grace of God and the free gift by the grace of that one man Jesus Christ abounded for many."*

However, Christ was not conceived through normal sexual relations. He was conceived by the Holy Spirit, which means that no man's "seed" entered into the woman (Mary) to enable the conception of Jesus. God, through the Holy Spirit, entered into Mary and made possible that which is not biologically possible (i.e. being conceived without the "seed" of a man), allowing Jesus to be conceived, born, and live a sinless life as no sin nature was imputed to Him since He had no physical father like we do.

Matthew 1:18-23 (KJV) - *"Now the birth of Jesus Christ was on this wise: When as his mother Mary was espoused to Joseph, before they came together, she was found with child of the **Holy Ghost**. Then Joseph her husband, being a just man, and not willing to make her a public example, was minded to put her away privily. But while he thought on these things, behold, the angel of the Lord appeared unto him in a dream, saying, Joseph, thou son of David, fear not to take unto thee Mary thy wife: for that **which is conceived in her** is of the **Holy Ghost**. And she shall bring forth a son, and thou shalt call his name Jesus: for he shall save his people from their sins. Now all this was done, that it might be fulfilled which was spoken of the Lord by the prophet, saying, Behold, **a virgin** shall be with **child**, and shall bring forth a son, and they shall call his name Emmanuel, which being interpreted is, God with us."* - (emphasis mine)

Did you notice what it says? She was a virgin when she conceived. Physically that's impossible, especially in those times. But with God, all things are possible. So by His being conceived of the Holy Spirit, the "seed" that was given to the woman (Mary) was sinless and flawless, and thus no sin nature was found in Him (Jesus). This part is important as you'll see later on. So why did Jesus, the Son of God, have to be born sinless, clothed in flesh, and made to come here only to suffer and die? As usual, I'll let the Bible answer that for me.

Romans 3:23 (KJV) - *"For all have sinned, and come short of the glory of God;"*

Once again we come back around to the fact that all

6

have sinned, that we live in moral depravity, with sins as dark and evil as the most vile things you can think of, and then some. And what is the result of this sinful, moral depravity?

Romans 6:23 (KJV) - *"For the **wages** of sin is **death**; but the gift of God is **eternal life** through **Jesus Christ** our Lord."* (emphasis mine)

The cost of our sin, the "wages" we earn through the commission of sin, is death, both physical and spiritual.

Romans 5:12 (KJV) - *"Wherefore, as by one man sin entered into the world, and death by sin; and so death passed upon all men, for that all have sinned:"*

Are you starting to see the picture here? By sinning we bring death upon ourselves. And if we are hopelessly sinful, what hope do we have of being saved from the just and righteous requirement of making payment for our sins? For every sin we commit an act of restitution must be made in turn. But if we are sinful and finite, such an act becomes impossible for us. So who or what can pay for our sins, to wash away our iniquity, our guilt, our shame, our wretchedness?

CHRIST DIED FOR US

Since sins, according to God's law, MUST, by necessity, be paid for, that leaves but one option for us. Eternity in Hell: the most horrible, terrible, fearful place in all of creation, and the one and only proper payment for what we have done. Or is it? What if there was another way, a scapegoat if you will, that could take away our punishment and set us free from the penalty of our sins? One such person exists.

Isaiah 53:5-6 (KJV) - "*But he was wounded for our transgressions, he was bruised for our iniquities: the chastisement of our peace was upon him; and with his stripes we are healed. All we like sheep have gone astray; we have turned everyone to his own way; and the Lord hath laid on him the iniquity of us all.*"

Romans 5:6, 8 (KJV) - "*6 For when we were yet without strength, in due time Christ died for the ungodly. 8 But God commendeth his love toward us, in that, while we were yet sinners, Christ died for us.*"

Jesus Christ *IS* our scapegoat. He came to Earth knowing that we had no other way by which to be saved. So He willingly gave His own sinless, perfect life for us that we might be saved and set free. Yes, Jesus took it all. He took every one of our sins, and every ounce of God's wrath and punishment, the very punishment we deserve, onto Himself. As such all of our sins were taken off of us and put onto Him. That doesn't make us immediately sinless, as we still have our fleshly sin nature, but it does take away the eternal punishment and imprisonment in Hell for our sins that we so rightly deserve.

And since Jesus was both God, and sinless, He had no sins of His own that He would be accountable for. Therefore He was completely free to take all of our sins upon Himself in willing payment for all the evil and wickedness we have done before God. But to do this Jesus had to die, taking our punishment of death and Hell upon Himself, forever imputing His righteousness upon us through this act of sacrifice. But if that were all He did, the work would be incomplete, and Jesus would not be God. So what other act did Jesus do that completed this sin transaction?

JESUS ROSE AGAIN!

Luke 24:1-7 (KJV) - "*Now upon the first day of the week, very early in the morning, they came unto the sepulchre, bringing the spices which they had prepared, and certain others with them. And they found the stone rolled away from the sepulchre. And they entered in, and found not the body of the Lord Jesus. And it came to pass, as they were much perplexed thereabout, behold, two men stood by them in shining garments: And as they were afraid, and bowed down their faces to the earth, they said unto them, Why seek ye the living among the dead? He is not here, but is risen: remember how he spake unto you when he was yet in Galilee, Saying, The Son of man must be delivered into the hands of sinful men, and be crucified, and the third day rise again.*"

In order to complete our Salvation, Jesus not only had to die on the cross of Calvary, but He also had to rise from the grave! Why was resurrection so important to our Salvation? Well, part of it was symbolic, the dying of the old man (sinful) and the raising up of the new man (sinless), and part of it was literal, namely the taking of death and Hell captive, freeing us from the penalty of our sins and giving us eternal life with God. So if sin brought death, the death of Jesus brought us life, and that far more abundantly, and eternal. So how does one receive this payment for sins? Clearly, if people are still going to Hell today, the payment for our sins is not automatic.

While they have indeed been paid for, one must understand that Salvation is a gift, and as a gift it must be received first before it can be our own. So how does one go about receiving this gift? How does one become saved from the penalty of their sins?

TRUST IN HIM
(I.E. ACCEPT HIM AS MY SUBSTITUTE)

To receive this gift, as with any gift, you must first accept it. No gift is yours, no matter what it is, until it is accepted. So how does one accept this gift? Some call it the "sinner's prayer", or the "prayer of Salvation". In reality it's merely your act of acceptance for something that has already been made yours, but has not yet been received by you. A simple sinners prayer begins by you acknowledging your sins. Confess them to God, then ask for His forgiveness. Acknowledge that you understand that Jesus died and rose again from the dead for your sins, and to save you, and that you freely accept His (Jesus Christ's) gift to you, and you accept Him as your Lord and Savior, and for Him to come into your heart and life and take over completely.

Now I can't just write this for you. This isn't something you recite verbatim and hocus pocus you're saved. It doesn't work that way. This is best done in *your own words*, and it must be honest, heartfelt, and legitimate. It can't be insincere and flippant. You *must* truly mean what you say. If it's not sincere, then it's just a bunch of words and the gift will still not be yours. This has to be an actual, honest, true request to God. You must _WANT_ Jesus in your heart and life and not just a "get out of jail free" card, so to speak. We're not doing magic here. This is an actual, true, honest spiritual transaction. By doing this you are willingly handing over your entire life to Jesus and in turn He will give you freedom from the penalty and guilt of your sins, and eternal life as a result.

As I said, I can't do this for you. It's something YOU must do for yourself, and it must be honest and legitimate. I can't stress that enough. You can't fake your way through this. God knows if you're honest or not. He knows your heart right down to the tiniest fiber of your being. He knows every single atom in your body. Trust me, for someone who knows that much, you can't in your wildest dreams hope to deceive Him. If it's not legit, you gain nothing but a false title at best, and probably a deeper, darker corner of Hell at the very worst. So you must really, really want this.

SO WHAT IS A CHRISTIAN?

So up to this point you've likely been wondering where I'm going with all of this. If you're reading this, and have made a decision to follow Christ, praise the Lord for you are now a Christian! But if you've never accepted Christ as your Lord and Savior, you are still lost in your sins and on your way to Hell. However, that still doesn't answer the question of what is a Christian? Or does it? Look back at what I just wrote above and think about it. Everyone is a sinner, right? Then we're all the same, despite our differences. We're all sinners. Then what makes a Christian different or unique from the average person? For the sake of argument let's assume the average person is unsaved and going to Hell, whereas a Christian is saved through the sacrifice of Jesus and Heaven bound. With that in mind, what constitutes being a Christian?

THE TRANSFORMATION VS CONDEMNATION

The first thing that happens when a person is saved and accepts Jesus Christ as Lord and Savior, is that they are transformed. What does that mean? The Bible speaks of a spiritual transformation that occurs at the point of Salvation. It describes this transformation as becoming "A new creation", or as Christ said, that person becomes "born again", hence the widely used term within Christianity. Some have even described this transformation as God taking a person's heart of stone and giving them a heart of flesh, spiritually speaking.

2 Corinthians 5:17 (KJV) - *"Therefore if any man be in Christ, he is a new creature: old things are passed away; behold, all things are become new."*

John 3:3-6 (KJV) - *"Jesus answered and said unto him, Verily, verily, I say unto thee, Except a man be born again, he cannot see the kingdom of God. Nicodemus saith unto him, How can a man be born when he is old? can he enter the second time into his mother's womb, and be born? Jesus answered, Verily, verily, I say unto thee, Except a man be born of water and of the Spirit, he cannot enter into the kingdom of God. That which is born of the flesh is flesh; and that which is* *born of the Spirit is spirit."*

What is born of flesh, is flesh. But what is born of spirit, is spirit. What did Jesus mean by that? First you have to understand that it's a figure of speech describing the two states of mankind; both unsaved and saved respectively. It also describes one's physical birth, as well as one's spiritual birth at the moment of Salvation. But how is the latter possible? We all understand physical birth, but what is spiritual birth? I believe the great author CS Lewis probably answered this question best when he said, "You are not a body with a soul. You **are** a soul. You **have** a body." The real us, the person who we actually are, is NOT this body. That is merely a house or shell inside of which lives our soul, the real us. As a house is only temporary, so is this body. At some point it will die and be put into the grave. But the real us will continue on throughout eternity.

For the unsaved, that eternity will be spent first in the fires of Hell, and then later in the Lake of Fire. Hell is only a holding pen for those who've rejected Jesus Christ as Savior. The Lake of Fire on the other hand, as spoken of in Revelation, is the eternal home of the lost, and a great deal worse than Hell. And those who will find themselves in that horrible place aren't there because God just wanted to be mean. God is holy and righteous, and as His creations we are beholden to Him.

Therefore, if we sin, we must pay the penalty for that sin, as described earlier in this thesis. But we also have a free will, and if we choose to reject God and want nothing to do with Him, He will honor that request. Yes, that seems a bit strange, but by sinning against God we are telling God we don't want His will, or Him for that matter. We are very clearly saying we want our own will, our own way, and we want nothing to do with God. Satan and the fallen angels said the same.

They said, "Our will, not yours." That's what Hell is. It is a place in which that request is answered. That is the place where all those who wish to be devoid of God and His will are sent. As such it is also a place completely devoid of God. That's what makes it the horrible nightmare that it is. Hell is a place where God does not reside. As such, evil reigns supreme. That's one of the reasons it's so horrible. As there is no God, there is no light, no peace, no safety, no joy, no good, no love, no beauty, no freedom, no rest. Basically, all things that are of God are absent. But all the things of evil are present and in great quantities, causing in turn great suffering, heartache, and loss.

Heaven on the other hand is a place where God rules, and His will is supreme, and Heaven is a paradise of spectacular and unimaginable beauty, peace, tranquility, love and more. And before you wonder too much why I'm off on this little rabbit trail, continue reading an you'll see my logic in going down this path. First off, let's look at Heaven and all it's beauty. In a sense Heaven is the physical embodiment of all that God is. God is love, so Heaven is filled with love. God is light, and in turn Heaven is filled with light. God is our provider, and in Heaven there is no want of anything. Whatever righteous thing your heart desires, that is there in plenty.

Now, contrast that with the saved believing Christian vs someone lost in the world. Those who are lost and unsaved, who have not turned to Jesus in repentance, and said, in essence, "Thy will be done" (think: sinners prayer) have been left to their own will and devices. It is a life completely devoid of God and, while that life may start out well, it eventually sinks into Hell, both figuratively and literally. However, when Jesus fully takes ownership of someone's heart and life, the transformation is not only noticeable. It's unmistakable. There is quite literally a transformation from darkness into light. The darkness, albeit spiritual in this case, is when someone is lost and without Christ.

The light is when Jesus, the second member of the godhead, comes into one's heart and soul and washes away the darkness that filled it in the time before Salvation. So this action quite literally transforms one from darkness into light, and also adds in all the things that were not there before. This is the essence of what spiritual birth is; going from death (darkness) into life (light). And yet it's so much more than this, far more than words can describe. Sure, we can know a shadow of the things that God will bring into our lives before we're saved. But we can't know them to any degree like we do once Jesus resides in our hearts. Or at least not to the extent we will after we're saved. The life one lives on both sides of Salvation also reflects this. Where one was predisposed to do evil before Salvation, one quickly becomes repulsed by its mere mention or the thought of it once they are saved. This, as well as other similar behaviors, are what believers call the "fruit" of the individual, the next clue in what it means to be a Christian.

THE FRUIT OF SALVATION

Matthew 7:16-20 (KJV) - "*By their fruit you will recognize them. Do people pick grapes from thornbushes, or figs from thistles? Likewise, every good tree bears good fruit, but a bad tree bears bad fruit. A good tree cannot bear bad fruit, and a bad tree cannot bear good fruit. Every tree that does not bear good fruit is cut down and thrown into the fire. Thus, by their fruit you will recognize them.*"

While the original context of these verses from Matthew 7 is in regards to false prophets, the statement still applies to everyone as a whole. Your "fruit", aka your actions, reveal many things about you. In fact, they tell so much about you that if someone is astute enough they can tell you your entire life's story simply by observing the way you live and express yourself. This in turn plays back on the previous topic of transformation. One way to tell if an individual is truly transformed is to look at how they treat others. Those who are unsaved tend to be selfish and self-centered in nature. Even their love is selfish, greedy, and conditional in nature. i.e. you make me happy, I make you happy. Those who have been saved tend to be God centered, and thus their nature in turn is focused toward others rather than themselves. Now sure, there are unsaved who are selfless, and saved who are selfish, but in general the unsaved tend to be naturally selfish and the saved naturally selfless without question.

Galatians 5:22-23 (KJV) - *"But the fruit of the Spirit is love, joy, peace, longsuffering, gentleness, goodness, faith, meekness, temperance: against such there is no law."*

If you've ever wondered what the "fruits" of a born again believer are, you only need take a look at the above verse. Another good one comes from 1st Corinthians and is sometimes referred to as the "Love Chapter" given it's beautiful description of what love truly is.

1 Corinthians 13:4-7 (NIV) - *"Love is patient, love is kind. It does not envy, it does not boast, it is not proud. It does not dishonor others, it is not self-seeking, it is not easily angered, it keeps no record of wrongs. Love does not delight in evil but rejoices with the truth. It always protects, always trusts, always hopes, always perseveres."*

For the believer this is an incredible verse to recite and memorize. It's really useful. One example I've used personally, and seen other use, is to recite this verse to oneself daily. It helps the believer stay mindful of how they should be if they want to be Christ like. Sure, the Bible contains a LOT of examples of what and who Christ was and how He acted. But this, one could say, is all of that wrapped up in a small, easy to remember package. It's also a great way to help you evaluate someone to tell if they are truly walking in the footsteps of Christ or, if they claim to be a Christian, if they are lying and perhaps even living a hypocritical life.

Obviously nobody lives this perfectly. But a true Christian will live nearly 100% of this every day of their lives.

So how does one go about using this as a litmus test for themselves, or even someone else to test and evaluate their walk with Christ? Simply replace "Love" and "It" with someone's name, including your own, and then be brutally honest with the evaluation. For example, let's say you're talking with someone named "John". You'd take this verse and render it like this:

"John is patient, John is kind. John does not envy, John does not boast, John is not proud. John does not dishonor others, John is not self-seeking, John is not easily angered, John keeps no record of wrongs. John does not delight in evil but rejoices with the truth. John always protects, always trusts, always hopes, always perseveres."

If you can recite that verse either over someone else, or even over yourself, with the your name or the names of others inserted into their respective places within the verse, and you can't honestly say that such things are true either of yourself or the other person, then they or you are not living as Christ did. I'm not saying it's easy. I've been a Christian for 23 years and I'm still struggling at this. And even though this isn't the complete guild to living as a Christian, it is pretty much the complete outward expression of what's in your heart in a nutshell.

If you're unsaved it doesn't give you something to aspire to. It gives you an idea of what you will become naturally once Jesus resides within your heart. And if you do claim to be saved, the elements of this verse should flow from your heart and life as naturally as water from a mountain spring. If not, then you need to get your life set in order, and do some serious repenting and getting your life right before God.

A FRUITFUL EXAMPLE

One great example of the transforming power of Jesus Christ comes from a good friend of mine named Richie. I remember the first day he came to church. It started out as an average Sunday and become an extremely memorable day. One of the elders, Vic I believe, had been inviting him to come to Church over and over and over again for years. But Richie kept refusing. Finally, one Sunday morning he decided to take Vic up on the offer. So in he rolls, a dirty old man, both quite literally and spiritually, covered in concrete dust and filled with a filthy, sin soaked spirit. And I'm not being mean. He'll admit the same thing. He came in reeking of sin so badly that you could feel it all the way across the aisle. Yet that morning, when I looked at him from my pew across the way, I felt deep concern and pity for him, and quietly lifted up a prayer for A Fruitful Example

One great example of the transforming power of Jesus Christ comes from a good friend of mine named Richie. I remember the first day he came to church. It started out as an average Sunday and become an extremely memorable day. One of the elders, Vic I believe, had been inviting him to come to Church over and over and over again for years. But Richie kept refusing. Finally, one Sunday morning he decided to take

Vic up on the offer. So in he rolls, a dirty old man, both quite literally and spiritually, covered in concrete dust and filled with a filthy, sin soaked spirit. And I'm not being mean. He'll admit the same thing. He came in reeking of sin so badly that you could feel it all the way across the aisle. Yet that morning, when I looked at him from my pew across the way, I felt deep concern and pity for him, and quietly lifted up a prayer for God to reach him.

And God did! Richie came in a filthy sinner and left a saint! Admittedly he was still a man that needed much sanctification, but even so he left transformed none the less. Then, over the next several months you could see a transformation in Richie that was absolutely amazing! The once dirty old man become a wonderful gentle giant who loved the Lord in ways that would make me jealous were it possible. In only a couple weeks the difference between his old and new self was like night and day! Within a very short time you saw nothing but smiles on his face and joy in his step!

That was the first big noticeable change. Another was his language. He went from cursing God to praising Him. He got himself a bible, got discipled, came regularly to church, and so much more. And this same man, who in all his previous years of life, refused to darken the doorstep of any church for any reason whatsoever, save perhaps for weddings and funerals. This simple, now redeemed and Godly man, is an excellent example of the transformation that comes with Salvation. The old man (or woman) is reborn and made new, and the fruits of their life show it! And boy, does Richie show it! If you want to see the joy of the Lord pouring out of someone, he's about as textbook an example as you'll find these days!

And God did! Richie came in a filthy sinner and left a saint! Admittedly he was still a man that needed much sanctification, but even so he left transformed none the less. Then, over the next several months you could see a transformation in Richie that was absolutely amazing! The once dirty old man become a wonderful gentle giant who loved the Lord in ways that would make me jealous were it possible. In only a couple weeks the difference between his old and new self was like night and day! Within a very short time you saw nothing but smiles on his face and joy in his step!

That was the first big noticeable change. Another was his language. He went from cursing God to praising Him. He got himself a bible, got discipled, came regularly to church, and so much more. And this same man, who in all his previous years of life, refused to darken the doorstep of any church for any reason whatsoever, save perhaps for weddings and funerals. This simple, now redeemed and Godly man, is an excellent example of the transformation that comes with Salvation. The old man (or woman) is reborn and made new, and the fruits of their life show it! And boy, does Richie show it! If you want to see the joy of the Lord pouring out of someone, he's about as textbook an example as you'll find these days!

What Does it Mean to be a Christian

STILL SINFUL OR STILL A SINNER?

Now, the next question to ask yourself is, do Christians still sin? Well, let me in turn ask you this. Are we still flesh and blood like everyone else? Yes. Just because one's heart is changed doesn't mean the body is changed, nor the sin nature removed. What it means is that the sin nature, the natural urge to commit sin, while still present, is no longer the ruling force in one's life. It's still there like an annoying relative that won't go away. Even so, it no longer runs your life. Jesus is now in charge of that. The sin nature simply sticks its nose in things from time to time (where it's absolutely not wanted) and causes trouble. Even so, does that make us sinful or a sinner? Well, to determine that we first have to define what each means.

Being sinful, by definition, is being filled with or having a nature towards sin. Being a sinner, on the other hand, is being one who expresses or commits sin. A great analogy of this can be expressed through the concept of a watering can vs a gardener. One is filled with water, the other expresses it by pouring out that water. Both those who are saved and those who are not are by nature sinful, as we are filled with an inherited sin nature coming from all the way back to Adam in much the same way that the watering can is full of water. As such all are naturally sinful. But it's not until we are saved that we give up the desire to be sinful. That doesn't mean we won't sin. Everyone sins, as that's our nature. But the urge to willfully express it is driven out of us by the redeeming power of Christ.

Think again of the example of the gardener. When we are in charge of our lives, before our hearts are transformed, we are the ones who express the sin that exists within our nature. But once Christ comes into our lives, as He is THE Gardener, and not A gardener, He places His hand upon ours, and through time removes that native urge to express our sin, instead creating a desire in us to instinctively restrain that sin nature. So while it's a progressive transformation that won't see complete fulfillment until we are removed from our bodies and given a new, renewed, transformed body that is devoid of the sin nature, as time goes on the believer becomes less and less drawn to commit sin.

So to answer the question, are we still sinful or a sinner once we are saved, I think the answer is yes to both. But, where an unsaved person expresses their sin naturally, a Christian by nature restrains it within themselves through the power of the Holy Spirit, seeking to sin less and less each day, ever striving forward towards sinless perfection. Part of this is because Jesus said, "Be like Me", and as anyone knows, Jesus was the perfect, sinless Son of God. As such we are commanded to be like Christ in nature, and that means always moving upwards towards sinless perfection and perfect love. And even though such sinless perfection is not possible in this life, it doesn't mean we don't try. And we're not doing it to be self-righteous. We're doing it in obedience and gratitude to the one who saved us from our sins. After all, why would you want to continue doing something you've been saved from and forgiven for?

PART OF A FAMILY

Being a Christian is being more than just a saved, born again follower and servant of Jesus Christ, the Son of God. It is being part of a very, very special, and exceptionally large family.

Matthew 12:46-50 (KJV) - *"While he yet talked to the people, behold, his mother and his brethren stood without, desiring to speak with him. Then one said unto him, Behold, thy mother and thy brethren stand without, desiring to speak with thee. But he answered and said unto him that told him, Who is my mother? and who are my brethren? And he stretched forth his hand toward his disciples, and said, Behold my mother and my brethren! For whosoever shall do the will of my Father which is in heaven, the same is my brother, and sister, and mother."*

Being a part of this family does not necessarily require being related by blood. Only by spirit. As we are all of the same Lord and God, we are all one kindred people, even if we are born of different blood, for it is the spirit that is the true us, and not this fleshly veil we wear every day. I'm sure it's a comfort to know that the real us can't grow old, get wrinkly, get gray hair, go blind, go deaf, lose a leg, and so on. So if this body is merely a house, it only stands to reason that family is not flesh and blood, but rather a spiritual tie that binds one to another. This can be seen in the example of adoption.

If I were to adopt a child, legally they would become mine as soon as I signed the adoption papers, and immediately would become my son or daughter, even though they are of no blood relation to me. At that moment that child would cease to be an orphan and would become my child for life. Even if I had a wife who bore me other children, actual sons and daughters of my own flesh and blood, that adopted child would have no less place in my family or my heart than if they were born into my family. That is what it's like to be saved. You're reborn spiritually, and in doing so you're adopted by Christ, or as some would say, "Born into the family of God." And in the same way I'd love that adopted child as one of my own, Christ loves us the same, and a billion times more.

So if you're a fellow Christian, you're family. That doesn't mean God doesn't love the sinner too. It instead means that God loves the Christian as a father would love their child, and so much more. It's a love that is true, unconditional, and without bounds or limits. It doesn't mean He won't hold the sinner accountable for their sins. But it does mean that He loved, and still loves, us so much that He sent Jesus to Earth to suffer and eventually die in our place so that we might be reconciled to Him. Yes, His love is that great. It's that same family relationship that many children already know, but on nitro. And once you are adopted into the family of God you are forever a son or daughter of the King, and you will never be an orphan or outcast again!

NOT A RELIGION

The word "Religion" is an interesting term within the English language that carries a multitude of meanings with it. To some it means that you believe in, worship or celebrate something of importance that sits at the center of your life and rules all of your decisions, actions, practices, and more. To others it's an excuse to do horrible things to other people in the name of an individual or ideology. But the correct understanding of the term "religion" is that it's man's attempt to reach God.

If you research all the religions of the world, from Hinduism to Buddhism, from Secular Humanism to Atheism, from Earth worship to Occultism, they all have the same central theme which drives their observance and practice. Even Secular Humanism and Atheism which, while denying that any god exists, including Jehovah God Himself, has made a god out of science, self, and the human body, or any of a variety of things in nature, and in some cases even nature itself. So by their own admission they are attempting to reach God, even if their god is one of their own making.

But whereas man created religions only change the

actions of the individual, Salvation in Jesus Christ changes the heart of the person, making them an entirely new creation. And, as stated on the previous page, it's also a family, and thus a relationship, whereas religion is merely a collection of observants of a defined set of beliefs, be that observation willful, or unwillingly as in some cases. Therefore, as stated before, Christianity is a relationship with the very God who created us, whereas religion is nothing more than the following of a predetermined set of rules in hopes of reaching God. i.e. I must do this and this if I am to *earn* my way to Heaven. Christianity says that Salvation is only through Jesus Christ, and His death and resurrection. Religion says, "do this and you will go to Heaven". As Christians, the only action we are required to do is to accept the finished work of Jesus Christ as payment for all our sins. Religion tries to atone for the sins of the observant through "good" works through man's own power, which is in and of itself utterly pointless given that even our good works are vile before God.

Religion says do. Christ says accept. Religion says there is much to be done. Christ says, "It is finished." Religion says it is not guaranteed. Christ says it is of a certainty. Religion points towards what man must be. Christ points to what He already is. Religion says there are many ways. Christ says there is only one way, namely Himself. Religion says hate your enemies. Christ says love your enemies. Religion says "Do this." Christ says, "Be transformed." So in the end, Christianity is entirely separate and unique from the religions of men, and it is in no way a religion. It is a relationship of the highest order with the very God who created us.

LOVE LIKE NO OTHER

One of the most powerful things about a true Christian is their love. But it's not actually their love we're seeing, but rather the love of Christ shining through them. To understand this, think of how we speak of children and some of the things they do. "You smile just like your father." "You have your mother's laugh." "You're a fisherman just like your uncle!" It's little phrases like that which help identify little imperfect traits within the child that emulate stronger, more defined traits of other people whom they've been near. In the same way that certain personality traits and attitudes of the parents shine through their children, Jesus in turn shines through us. Since, through Salvation, we are adopted into His family, we in turn begin to emulate His personality to others.

It goes along with the old saying that "The only Jesus some people will ever see is the one they see in you." In other words, if someone is truly saved and following the example of Christ, people around them will get a taste of what Jesus is like by observing their behavior. In the same way that children emulate their parents, believers emulate Jesus and all that He is. Not His deity obviously, but rather His characteristics. One of those is love. And not just any love. The Greeks called it "Agape", which we would understand to mean "unconditional love". This is a love that is without requirements, limits, boundaries or borders, and is changeless, unmovable and unshakable. It's a love that goes from everlasting to everlasting and is eternal, meaning it never ends.

And while we can't hope, in our limited, finite, fallen state, to express such a love in its entirety, we can offer a small taste of that to those around us. But even that tiny grain of love that we try our best to emulate seems so massive and unrealistically powerful to the average person. So much so even that it seems to be beyond understanding to them. How can one hope to understand the fullness of God's love, be it from the Father, Jesus, the Holy Spirit, or any combination of the three, when one lives in a world that, by nature, is devoid of love because of sin? There *are* some things we can call love in this world. But they are more along the lines of what would be described as selfish or self-interested love. i.e. you fill this and that criteria and I *might* love you.

In other words, "I will *appear* to love you so long as it's to my advantage. The moment it ceases to be, I will abandon you to the dogs." But Christ's love says, "I will rescue you out of your sin and depravity, no matter what it costs me." Think about that. Jesus loved us so much that He came to Earth, something He had no reason to do, save that He loved us unconditionally and didn't want to see us lost or cast into Hell forever. The untold, unimaginable suffering He went through just to save us is beyond human words to describe. But was it selfish? Was it a situation where He said, "I want them for my own pleasure and therefore I will suffer greatly and die for them"?

Selfishness doesn't put others before itself. It's entirely a self-centered viewpoint. To put yourself out there sacrificially just to satisfy your own needs goes entirely against the nature of what selfishness is. Love on the other hand is putting others before yourself. But you might still say, "Yes, but look at all that Jesus gained!" Perhaps. But at the same time look at all that Jesus lost. Yes, He will save some from this world to be His own people. But inversely He will lose so many more. One theologian stated that the ratio of those who will go to Hell vs those who will find Heaven is a thousand to one. I don't know if that number is right, but even so, think about that. Selfishness, which is ultimately spawned from greed, which in turn is spawned from pride, all of which are sins that God is not capable of committing, follows the law of conservation.

That law is the foundation on which all of life is centered. It states basically that each creature will, by nature, seek to gain the most benefit from whatever they are doing through the least amount of cost or expenditure on their part. In economic terms, we say that we want to get the most "bang for our buck" or "expend the least number of dimes while gaining the greatest number of dollars." Basically it's our natural desire to spend the least amount of money to gain the maximum amount of profit or value. Yet Christ gave everything, and still has come away with less than what He spent. He died for EVERYONE and poured out Himself completely, and yet in the end He will lose a majority of those He sought to save. That's not selfishness in the slightest. That is pure love; a love beyond limit, comprehension, or understanding, a love like no other, willing to expend more than it takes in, sow more than it reaps, gives more than it receives. That is what Agape means. Unlimited, unconditional, unselfish love. Or as the title says, it's a "love like no other."

PEACE LIKE NO OTHER

One of the things that still fascinates me about the Christian life, even after nearly 24 odd years into my walk with Christ, is the incredible, unbelievable peace that fills my life. As a child and growing up through my teen years, one of the things that constantly pervaded my life was fear. I was always constantly fearful and afraid. To make matters worse I had, undiagnosed at that time, ADHD (which evolved into ADD) and Asperger's (a high functioning form of autism), all combined with the social awkwardness that only a nerdy, geeky, introverted person can fully understand. I was literally terrified of others and my surroundings. Even now I still struggle with what they call agoraphobia. i.e. a fear of crowds. If you stuck me in a crowd of other people I very easily became scared and awkward in some pretty predictable ways. But put me on stage and I'd just about come unglued.

That fear always pervaded my life, filled me with anxiety, and drove who I was. Oddly enough, it was that fear which also drove me to the altar and lead me to Christ. So while mostly bad, it did have its good points. But what intrigued me the most, and still does to this day, is that moment of Salvation when Jesus came into my heart. Like a flood of cleansing water, a peace that passes all understanding flooded over me and washed the fear out of my heart. For the first time in my entire life I actually felt peace. Not just a temporary peace or a "you're safe" kinda peace. This was a peace that had no rhyme or reason. It was a peace that looked fear straight in the eye and laughed. Or danger for that matter. But it wasn't a kind of peace that laughed at danger, and said, "Bring it on!" This was one that said, "No matter what happens, it will be alright."

I couldn't explain it, nor understand it. How could I be standing there staring death in the face and yet have this incredible, unbelievable, overwhelming peace in my heart!? To the human mind it makes absolutely no sense. But if you factor God into the equation, now it starts becoming a little more understandable. But even then it's still a peace that passes all understanding. And that's not a cliché statement either! That's really what you're feeling! And I look back on my life before Christ and compare it to now, and it's like night and day. Not because I got saved, or became a better person, or because Christ filled my heart. All of those are important, so don't think I'm relegating them to second place. Not in the slightest! But when you look at the incredible peace that came into my life on that day I got saved, wow. I still remember getting up from the altar and sitting down in my pew with the biggest smile ever crossing my face.

But it was the peace that I remember the most; that feeling in my heart of peace beyond understanding. The fear was gone, my sins had been forgiven, and from now on nothing would ever be wrong again. Yes, life would still be rough, and there would still be trials, heartache and pain. But no matter what, God would be with me, and His peace would follow me wherever I went. In fact, that peace in those early years was so strong that it gave me strength and courage like never before. In fact, that brings to mind an incident that occurred on one typical day in the mess hall. While I was serving in the army I worked as a cook, and in our mess hall we had a black staff sergeant who absolutely hated my guts. I mean, really, really, really hated my guts. He did everything he could to make my life miserable. I admit, some of it I deserved as I wasn't the brightest bulb in the box when it came to being a good soldier, but most of it I didn't. This hatred really bubbled to the surface one day while we were fixing lunch and exploded in my face as the most epic dressing down you've probably ever seen.

He went on a good ten or fifteen minute diatribe about how I was horrible, stupid, and every other name and insinuation you can think of, some of which were quite unmentionable. The thing is, I don't remember what he said, other than the fact that he was spewing a constant stream of vulgarity drenched in generous amounts of hatred and anger. Yet despite this, the single, most powerful, overwhelming memory of that incident was the incredible feeling of peace and God's presence that overflowed me that day. At the time this was something new to me, and I didn't quite know what to make of it at that moment. No matter how much vitriol the staff sergeant dumped on me, God's presence not only rebuffed it, but sent it packing. In fact, that feeling of peace was so overpowering I remember actually standing there grinning from ear to ear. Yeah, that probably didn't help the situation any because that REALLY made the sergeant mad.

Yet I couldn't help myself. God was there, and so was His peace that passes all understanding. But that wasn't the last time I felt His peace and love fill me and flow through me. There were many other times after that in which events unfolded in front of me with such ferocity and danger that it would have taken the heart of anyone who was not filled with the Spirit of God. That peace can take even something as terrifying as the end of the world, and allow you to walk through it in complete calmness and serenity without any fear or anxiety. That, in a nutshell, is the peace like no other.

Blessings Like No Other

Most religions around the world come with an ingrained blessings and rewards system. i.e. you do this and you will get that. Christianity even has that to some degree. We have some things, such as crowns (see 1 Cor. 9:24,25, 1 Thess. 2:19-20, Dan 12:3, James 1:12, 2 Tim. 4:8, 1 Pet. 5:1-4 for more information), which we earn as a result of what we do in this life. But unlike the religions of the world we immediately, upon getting saved, are given gifts. No religion that I know of can say that. With them you have to earn everything from your daily bread to your salvation. With Christianity, we are given gifts to begin our life with Christ as well as others all throughout our time on Earth, and even some when we get to Heaven. Some of this includes what we call "our daily bread", an antiquated term which means our daily provision of needs, be they physical or spiritual.

Another is spiritual gifts, which are special abilities or skills which are used to aid us in our work within the body of Christ, and with the tasks that we are to do for God. These include, but are not necessarily limited to, Prophecy, Helps (i.e. working for and helping others), Exhortation, Giving,

Leadership, Mercy, Words of Wisdom, Faith, Healing, Miracles, Discernment, Tongues (foreign, unknown languages) and the Interpretation of Tongues. These are discussed to some degree in Romans 12:6-8, 1 Corinthians 12:4-11, and 1 Corinthians 12:28 if you are interested in learning more. They are given to the new believer without the person asking or doing anything to earn them. They're a gift from God simply because you are now one of His children.

It's kinda the same idea as you moving into a new neighborhood. You no more than arrive with the first of your belongings and your neighbor shows up with a cake and a welcoming party. You didn't do anything to earn it, so why did they do it? Because you're now a neighbor. And as a father would give gifts to his children simply because they're his, God gives gifts to His children for the same reason, and also to help equip you for the ministry work that lies ahead of you. And these are gifts given for no other reason than because God is now your father and you are part of His family. Some might say, "But don't you earn those by Salvation?" I can understand where one would see that, but if the gifts you received were determinate on your Salvation, then your results could be repeatable and predictable. i.e. if I pray this way and I'm in this location, and I pray for salvation at this time and on this date, then I can get this and this gift.

It doesn't work that way. God decides what you get, how much you get, how many, and for how long. That means you can't earn it. Because if He controls the details, there's no earning of anything involved. That's why they're called gifts. But these aren't the only gifts that are given to us completely independent of our actions, including our daily provision.

Religions don't have that. To them, anything you get is something you've earned. But God gives spiritual gifts and Salvation without any effort on our part, save only for Salvation, and the only action we have to do there is to accept it. We never "earned" it, as it was a gift. It was only given and accepted, and nothing else, so there was no participation on our part. We only received what was already done. It's like someone giving you a truck. Did you build it? Did you design it? Did you put it together? Nope. You merely received the completed vehicle that someone else had already built.

That's the same idea with the gifts from God. But, as I stated above, they don't end at Salvation. We continue to be given gifts all through our lives. We're given sun and rain as they're needed, food and water, family, friends, work, resources, sickness and health, and so much more. Some of those might not seem like gifts. The sickness and rain for some would seem like curses. But we don't see things from God's viewpoint. We see our narrow little slice of time, but God sees all of eternity like a gigantic portrait. So if He sends us rain or sickness, just two of the things in life that some may call curses, then it's for a purpose. Let's take sickness for example. I know people who praise God for the sicknesses they've had in their lives. To them it was the one time in their life when they were the closest to God. During those sufferings and trials they drew close to God in ways they never did before, nor have since, much to their regret.

So in a way all of the troubles, trials, sickness, rain, tragedy, disaster and may other even worse things that happen in our life are actually gifts designed to draw us closer to God and stronger in our faith because, as nature has proven, it's not the perfect life that makes us stronger. It's our trials and struggles that strengthen us. So those are blessings and gifts from God to improve us. We never would have asked for them. Yet God knew we'd need them. And that's just the tip of what God gives to us, free of charge, often without our need to ask for them, and most definitely without our need to earn them. So in that, Christianity is a relationship with blessings like no other.

Only Scratching The Surface

While I've gone a long ways towards explaining much of what it means to be a Christian, I've only just begun to scratch the surface. If it took God the entire 66 books of the Bible to explain to us through examples, prophecies, teachings and a wide variety of other things what it means to be a true follower of God, how can I hope to do more than leave behind but a faint fingerprint of what it means to be a Christian? Really, the best way to understand what a true believer in Jesus Christ is, what they should be and what they are, is to begin at the book of Matthew and read the entire New Testament from cover to cover, and then flesh it out with the history, prophecy and teachings of the Old Testament. Because, while this is only the briefest of summaries on what it is to be a Christian, the Bible can do so much more to expand and improve your understanding of that, and of Jesus Christ, the Son of God.

Steven Lake

What Does it Mean to be a Christian

OTHER WRITINGS BY AUTHOR STEVEN LAKE

MANNA
Trusting in the Provisions of God

LOVE
God's Greatest Gift

THE GREAT COMMISSION
Answering God's Call To Missions

JENNA'S JOURNEY
A Journey To A New Beginning

.

www.ingramcontent.com/pod-product-compliance
Lightning Source LLC
Chambersburg PA
CBHW060720030426
42337CB00017B/2943